More Cat Psalms

More Cat Psalms

PRAYERS MY CATS HAVE TAUGHT ME

HERBERT BROKERING

Augsburg Books

MINNEAPOLIS

MORE CAT PSALMS
Prayers My Cats Have Taught Me

Copyright © 2008 Augsburg Books, an imprint of Augsburg Fortress. All rights reserved. Except for brief quotations in critical articles or reviews, no part of this book may be reproduced in any manner without prior written permission from the publisher. Visit www.augsburgfortress.org/copyrights/contact.asp or write to Permissions, Augsburg Fortress, Publishers, Box 1209, Minneapolis, MN 55440-1209.

Cover and book design: John Goodman and Michelle L. N. Cook
Cover and interior art: © Matthew L. Ambre/Artville

Library of Congress Cataloging-in-Publication Data
Brokering, Herbert F.
More cat Psalms : prayers my cats have taught me / Herbert Brokering.
  p. cm.
ISBN 978-0-8066-8035-4 (alk. paper)
1. Cat owners—Prayers and devotions. 2. Cats—Religious
aspects—Christianity. I. Title.
BV4596.A54B765 2008
242—dc22   2007037065

The paper used in this publication meets the minimum requirements of American National Standard for Information Sciences—Permanence of Paper for Printed Library Materials, ANSI Z329.48-1984.

Manufactured in the U.S.A.

12   11   10   09   08   2   3   4   5   6   7   8

Contents

Introduction — 9

Family — 12

Special — 14

Genes — 16

Time Off — 18

Special Meal — 20

Mine — 22

Chores — 24

Play — 26

Night Out — 28

I Like — 30

Stretch — 32

Diet — 34

I Sleep on It — 36

Make Well — 38

Tease — 40

Look at Me — 42

Satisfied — 44

Care — 46

Washing — 48

A Higher Being — 50

I Know My Place — 52

I Tread Lightly — 54

Talk to Me — 56

Good Morning — 58

I Believe — 60

Routine — 62

To my son Chris
who helped kittens grow into good cats

Introduction

God said: "Let there be cat."

What do cats have to do with God, spirit, prayer, creation, grace?

From childhood I knew cats are special in God's life with us. God made Cat and said: "This is very good." So a few years ago I wrote *Cat Psalms: Prayers My Cats Have Taught Me*, and thought that little book would be my one and only on cats. Thankfully, readers and publisher have asked for more. Cat lovers know there is always more and more to learn from a cat. So, *More Cat Psalms*.

The prayers in this particular volume focus on the meaning of grace. Now grace is a very large word and may come alive for you in these twenty-six prayers. While writing the prayers my mind's eye sees the cat world and all creation huddled, playing and living under the great umbrella of grace. May you grow in God's creational images of grace.

Attributes of God are one way to know God's complete presence in the world and in our lives. Incarnation brings God all the way into the universe and to every part of nature, cat, forest, brook, raindrop, breath, relationship, emotion—every thought, word, and deed. God is embedded in the all of life and all creation is imbedded in God. Emmanuel is an incarnate word; God is with us.

How easy to connect attitudes of God to attributes often evident inside a cat: "Look At Me . . . Care . . . I Know My Place . . . A Higher Being . . . I Tread Lightly . . . Good Morning . . . I Believe . . . Talk to Me."

God said, "Let there be Cat. And it was so." For this I am grateful. The attributes of Cat are what we too enjoy, feel, share, and depend on for life and well-being. Cat often reminds me of how God has created you and me to live a life of Grace. If you know a cat, look again.

More Cat Psalms will please cat lovers and help them look at Cat in a spiritual way. Creating Cat was God's intent to make a world "very good."

In my eighty-one years, I do not remember when we did not have a special tree or rock or cat. Creation keeps the spirit of God close to earth and incarnate.

Pray *More Cat Psalms* with friends, family, parish, sick, children, and those among you who are shut-in. God's spirit will take you beyond these twenty-six prayers as you look at creation all around.

Herbert Brokering

Family

I am cat. I am a member of your family. Once upon a time I came to live here. Was it by birth? Was I homeless? Did I appear at your door? Did you buy me? It does not matter; I am a member of the family. You call me by your family name. I eat and play and sleep here. I have my own bowl of food and my clean water dish. Sometimes I eat right beside you; you know how to set the rules. I am cat and we are family. You know where I nap and play and eat and cuddle and sleep. I know all your rooms for I have visited them when you were not home. You have told me which places are my own. They are enough. When company comes you introduce me. They answer and notice me for I am your cat. We are a gracious family.

God, *you fill me with family grace. I am family with homeless, with strangers, neighbors and with im-*migrants. I am at home with warring nations and political foes. Grace is my journey; I leave and I stray. Grace is how I find my way home. I know the power and joy of belonging. I know the helplessness and pain of being cut off from others. See me share my table, divide my abundance, give my time and extend my sense of household. Life is your gift to all. All share your one life and breath and spirit. You call us your children and so we are. As I have a safe place in your earth so may we all be family. God, at each dawn and dusk I find this place and all the earth a home of grace.*

Special

I am cat. I am special for you say I am. You call me pretty and beautiful and gorgeous and treat me with respect; so it is true. I am flattered and will not make you stop. You brush me even if I do not need brushing. You make me special without my asking. You show me to your friends and smile; they take turns holding me. I hear you when you mention my name by phone. You are glad at what they say. You look my way and smile. I cannot hear them but you keep turning to see me while they talk. I can tell you are proud, so I am proud. My cat-napper is homemade and matches your sofa. If I do not eat my food then you ask me what I want. I do not answer; you leave and return with something special. Some say I cost more than I am worth. You do not believe them. You treat me as a prize. I am your cat; I am special.

God, *your own grace is in me for you have made me in your own image. You formed me in my mother and* said I am very good; so I am. Some like my smile, some my eyes, my mind, my laugh; some like my spirit. How often my name is spoken for good. I am glad for those who know me, love me, and speak kindly of me. A banner was made when I was born; these are your words: "I have called you by my name." When I am down, when I do not seem to belong, then I am lifted up. I praise and thank you for you are gracious. I am more special than a cat cuddled in a cotton napper. It is so; I too am gracious, a member of your place of grace. You look my way and smile.

Genes

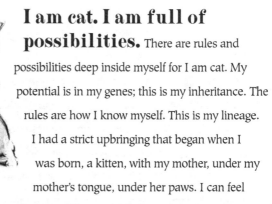

I am cat. I am full of possibilities. There are rules and possibilities deep inside myself for I am cat. My potential is in my genes; this is my inheritance. The rules are how I know myself. This is my lineage. I had a strict upbringing that began when I was born, a kitten, with my mother, under my mother's tongue, under her paws. I can feel every kindness, every washing; I still hear my mother's voice in coaching and warning me. I learned to fend for myself, to be cat in all ways. I learned to be quieter than fog, more still than breath. I can hear a mouse breathing from a distance. It is in my blood to listen. My mother did so; my father and my siblings did so. All cats did so before me. I know myself as cat, my kind of cat. When I came to live here did you Google and read about my pedigree, my genes, my nature, and me? You know what to expect. You have learned to want my kind of cat. Some of me is written in stone; some is written as in sand. I am cat; some of me is ageless, some is new. Grace is very old and is given.

God, *your grace is old; your grace is new. You have known me from the foundation of the world and yet I am like new each day. I have deep stories stored in old genes. Old grace is in me. My roots are alive; new twigs are budding. This is how you grow your grace. I am predictable as from old; I am new with surprise. The years of my life are in me; those who have held and fed and loved me have stayed in me. They are my story, begun in old times lived before me, a genetic pool from which I too drink. God, I have inherited a legacy of gifts that cannot be numbered. In me dwell codes and labels and markings that only you know. We Google, we research, we pray. We seek and we find. Grace permeates all creation, deep within and still unfolding. Wherever we go you are.*

Grace is truly present.

Time off

I am cat. I like time off, a break in the routine. A new hill to run, a new tree to climb, a different place to lie in the sun. To move around and find a nook I haven't stayed in for a while, or ever. Give me a dark corner, the sun light, a windowsill, under a porch, in the iris bed. Green leaves can be cool to lie on in a hot day. I need a mini vacation, a change of scenery, an evening stroll, a casual new friend, a confrontation, a risk, a scare, and a test to protect my rights. I need to see who lives next door, down the alley, and to know what is happening in the vacant building. I need time when no one touches me, or asks me to move, or runs a vacuum cleaner near me. I want time off where a corner is enough, when no one speaks to me, asks me to move, runs a sweeper near me, shouts to wake me. I am cat; give me some space. Grace is about personal space.

God, *all life is in motion. You have made us migrant, pilgrim, and curious seekers. Surprises are your great gift to us: a new neighbor, a site we never saw, a song we never heard, a new vacation spot. We have not met all our neighbors, or chosen all our friends, seen all our family, or visited all places we have promised each other. Jesus walked off into new places to find calm, to see clearer, to risk, to rest and to embrace what is new. We too prepare for the surprise of grace, space to be on our own. We explore, reach out, dig and reach places new. Grace is a wide circle in which to find a new place in the sun or a new nook on earth's great rug. I am not cat, but I take off to be surprised. I am not afraid for grace will follow me and then lead me home.*

Special meal

I am cat. Sometimes I need a special meal, a treat. I have watched your special meal times. You light a candle, I purr. You laugh. There is not always a plain reason for the meal but the smell of the meal is special. I am given seconds, thirds; a little more, something you know I like, a snack, a piece from your own plate. Food is special to me when you reach down to touch me as you give it, as though you prepared it for me. You surprise me and make me grand with food. The meal is special by the sound of your voice, the way you say my name when you hand me a morsel and the look in your eyes. You stand and watch me enjoy eating as though we are eating together. I smell the candle and I am sure it is lit for us. I feel gracious. I am cat and I need a special meal.

God, *your house of grace is filled with special meal times. You are host for one sip of wine, a piece of bread broken, a blessing given. Heaven and earth are at one table. A morning drink with a friend and you are there. A casserole beside a candle and the gathering is your banquet in a potluck. Hot cider at an open fire on a wintry night and heaven is here. How special are meals when served in your household. Summertime and gardens are rich with harvest. Trees bow down to be picked; again and again you give us first fruit of the season. One more meal is on the board, we gather to say grace. All food and drink is about grace. All creation eats at one table served by you, for you are in the world's one kitchen.*

O God, our food is about grace.

Mine

I am cat. My world is great for my size. Not everything I touch is mine; there is too much. I know what is mine. You have a chair you like best, I can tell. You sit at the same place when you eat. I need a place I know is for me, where you can look for me, pet me, talk to me. I need a place where my dish sets, my place. As a member of

the family I need a place that fits into this place we call home. I do not need to be chased, scolded, or frightened off. I do not like to be at the wrong dish. Let us decide together where is my welcome space. There are dishes I like but they are yours.

I know I am not allowed on the table or kitchen counter, though they smell good. I know all the places you say are mine and I am a wealthy cat. You help me to know that my world is very great and good. This is where I here you pray.

God, *so much is mine. You are generous and we have plenty. More and more I want to know how to* share your abundance. Skies and seasons and meadows and woods and gardens cannot be measured; they are plenteous. So much is mine to grow, to pick, to dig, to plant, to see, to view, to read, to sing, to take and to give. My dish is full. I have enough. In this place of grace I will share as you do. I will share my best bread, best drink, stories, walks, recipes, best thoughts, dreams, questions, and my best spirit. In this place of grace what is mine is also ours. All life is graceful, so we all break one bread on the one altar of grace. We will help to satisfy the hunger of every living thing.

God, your grace is very great for my size.

Chores

I am cat. I have chores. I roll over, you laugh. This is my work. I chase circles in the grass and leap for flying cattail seed while you take pictures. Jumping is my chore. My work is to humor others, to make you proud I am cat, to see you laugh while I do cat works. You boast to friends and feel exalted because of me. I have my own kinds of gifts which are my work. I keep you company, talk to you, listen, wake you, help you rest, calm you. It is easy to sleep near you, to lie at your feet and snuggle. I know some chores by heart, from birth. Some I am learning. You teach me to stay in my chair, go down stairs and find where to sleep. It is easy for me to create a habit, fit into the family and be dependable. I will take my place with you; let me know what you need, I will learn to please you. This is our place to live together, our part of the whole world. What I do I will do well. I am a full member of the family. I am responsible to you for I am cat.

God, *I too have chores. Some I know by heart; these I was born to do. Some are new which I am learning. There is work of grace to be done in the household of grace. Acts of mercy are tiny, some are great. The world needs caring. We do our work as work of grace: scrubbing, cooking, building, serving. Our good work is caring, hosting, saying goodbye, phoning, sending mail, looking in on a neighbor, checking a shut in, hearing a child's worry, enjoying a joke, wrapping a gift, preparing a party, sitting by a deathbed, singing a child to sleep. God, you give us chores of grace. My good works are how I played when little, and still play, shared and still do, cared and cuddled and still do, looked into a face while listening and still do, hurried to help and still do. God, my chores are the gifts you have given me to do and they are not done. I am not cat and cannot jump and tumble, yet, O God, my soul can leap and make others be more gracious.*

Play

I am cat. Where can I play? Do I get a tabletop? Can

I have a couch when I want? Can I have your bed when you are finished
sleeping? What belongs to me? What is yours? Help me know so I will not
feel wrong. When I romp I want to make you laugh, feel calm and be good
spirited. You have seen me walk, with grace, sit and be admired. I roll over
and you stop talking and laugh. I want to make you proud when company
comes. I can make a joke; I can be a clown. Where may I play? I will share
a yard or room with others. I must play, for I am cat and in me I want tall
trees to climb, logs to claw and earth to dig. In me I know swamps, stumps,
dusty paths and creeks to run. Help me find places to be playful and to
show the glad spirit in me. I am cat and need for us to play.

God, you have made us playful. Life begins with toys, surprises, rolling, running, throwing, catching, pretending, imagining, dreaming, believing. Life is playful. We are easily made glad; we quickly laugh and tease and surprise each other. We play peek-a-boo behind chairs and fingers and doors. We see and don't see. We pretend to hide and are glad. Years pass and we still play. We see and do not see; we understand and do not understand; we trust and do not trust. We play to hide and to be found. We know the joy of finding someone hid or lost. There is something in me I feel is playful: the way I tell stories, the kinds of questions I like, the twinkle in my eyes, my voice. Grace is playful. Grace knows every glad spirit.

Night out

I am cat. I need my night out. By myself, or with a friend, away, like a tiny vacation. A place to go and there to know what it's like to be cat. Off to be honest, silent, quiet, to ponder, risk, come what may. Nothing planned, a retreat, meditation, prayer. A time and place to look around look again, with other cats. To see what changed, out there and in me, a refresher course in Cat. A night for harmony, fitting it all together, ready to be me, a complete cat. To feel my strength, wit, agility, connections, and to admit my weakness, limits, boundaries. A little space to help get ready to come back, home, and stay forever. I need a time of grace to grow the cat in me.

God, *people of faith go off to a quiet place to pray. You have sung songs of the heart with singers, psalmists, mourners and prophets. You have raised up choirs and monasteries where a spirit can retreat. Forests and meadows and night skies and vistas are silent. We stand in them and you make us quiet. It is our night out, our day off, a vacation. Your grace heals, calms, quiets, ponders, meditates. Grace knows how we wander, that we risk, we stray, we are lost, we are called and we are brought home. God, your grace frees me to ask, seek and find what is new beyond and inside.*

Sometimes in dark times or in light days give me a night out.

I like

I am cat. There is so much I can do.

I like who I am. I am cat and that is who I wish to be. It is enough. I am not like all cats for there are cat choices. I learned early to like being cat with all my heart. I do what cats before me have always done, from their beginning. There is enough for me to do.

They say I have nine lives; there is a lot of life in me. Watch me and see what I can do. You will learn to know what I like, and I will know what you like. Listen to me purr; you will know what I like. We are not all the same; look at me, love me, pet me, feed me and you will know me. Show me what you like and what makes you glad. I purr. Life is good; it is enough. Show me you like who I am.

God, *I am full of life. My spirit overflows. Sometimes I go in all directions. My spirit expands, explodes, and bursts. I like who I am. I too chase circles and scramble tall trees and follow what I like. Then I come back, come down and am still, and I know who I am. There is so much to do; so you have made my world. There are new places I go; each place asks me to stay. My life is full of invitations; I am not bored. I listen, I hear, I go. This is my life and I like it. I listen to my head, I follow my heart. I go because it is not good to live alone. I go to feel their grace; I go to be graced. I will sacrifice; it may cost my life yet I go. I know what I like. I live a full life. Then I purr, O God, for I know where I am. I am home, full, fulfilled.*

Grace fills me with a full life.

Stretch

I am cat. I stretch when I wake. I do not know about health clubs and workouts but I have rules for being well. Doctors

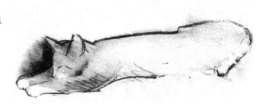

tell you to watch me wake and stretch when you get too busy. "Stretch like your cat," they say. Stretch. You come home from the hospital; I see you watch me. You stretch and yawn and roll your shoulders and bend your body like a willow. Like cats. You follow printed sheets; I follow a habit inside me I know from my beginning. I cannot read. I am cat, I stretch. I stretch and I feel greater than myself. Watch me; stretch. Together we know the feeling, the gift of stretching. There is life in me waiting to wake up inside me. I stretch; I yawn. I am cat.

God, *I stretch. I am more than the length in me. I stretch, my muscles waken. Now I am greater; my body wakes inside. Morning has dawned. I yawn. Morning keeps waking. A new day, a day full of grace. I feel a song; I know the gift of stretching, sinning into a new day. I stretch into the break of day and the end of day. I stretch and I feel strength in me, a cool breath; a healing spirit rushes through me like a summer breeze. I see the cat stretch. The nurse tells me, the doctor tells me; I read it in fliers: Stretch. The cat does it right. I watch the bird stretch. After a good rain green grass seems to stretch. There is a time to sleep and a time to stretch. I stretch and windows open in me. Dams break. Energy flows. Stress flees. In the simple act of stretching your grace is at work. May nations when uptight, too tense, then see a cat and stretch, stretch.*

Stretching is an exercise of grace.

Diet

I am cat. I know my diet. If my food doesn't come out of a can or plastic bag I know where to go, and I know my limit. I eat, I sleep, I wait, I run, I exercise, I climb, I eat; I rest, I ponder. I stretch, I plan, and I eat. There is an eating routine I follow; the plan is inside me. It was there from the beginning. I am tempted by foods that can only be found on food shelves. I join you at the table, at snack time, with leftovers, by begging through your kind spirit. I learn how you give in to me. I watch you at the microwave, at the refrigerator door and the cupboard. I know the sound of a paper sack. I smell what you bring in the shopping bag. I hear when a canister is opened; I can tell the snap of a cracker. I am cat and there is a desire in me, a plan and routine for eating that I obey. We do this together.

God, I sit to eat and say grace. We bless the whole table, the drinks, the salad and potatoes and fish and carrots and dessert. Let these gifts of grace be blessed. Cabbage, steak, broccoli, yams, tapioca pudding, we have it by your grace. Your earth and sun and rain grew the feast; farmers and migrants planted and picked the harvest. Merchants bought and sold it to me. The bounty is on the table: from the earth of Florida and Colorado and Chile and Mexico and California to the table. Ah, the route of grace. A meal of grace for health and strength. Ah, the power of aroma. Ah, the joy of a festive meal. Ah, the taste of a drink with a friend. Ah, the beauty of tomatoes and grapes on the vine. Ah, the taste of vintage wine. God, the groceries. The paper bags are full of first fruits. An offering sets on my table. Paper bags of food make my world of grace.

I sleep on it

I am cat. Sometimes I need time to decide, time to sleep on it. A good nap can make a big difference. A potential foe appears and I am ready for battle. You are near with a gentle word, a soft voice, and two strokes across my back, a smile. The foe is not an enemy; I am not ready to play, I am ready for a nap. I do not choose the warfare. When I wake I feel a more friendly world. I have slept off many battles I am glad were not waged. A nap is enough. I count to ten, go to a neutral corner, call time out. I sleep on it to change my mind. A morning can bring a brand-new day, create a new feeling and make me a new cat. I am cat. Give me time, a little time, to think it through. Grace needs time.

God, sometimes I sleep on it.

Not long, forty minutes, ten minutes, one hour; a little time of grace. It is more than time; it is the privilege, the gift of a few minutes to ponder and to pray. A little time of grace. It is enough. Minutes make a difference. I am glad for a few minutes before going on. I am glad to catch my breath in a long decision. I am glad to close my eyes when people gather for worship and to see ahead. I am glad to stay seated for the postlude and make a promise. Sometimes I need to sleep in, sit in and rest. I count to ten and then speak. God, in that tiny piece of time I feel your grace. I will be more careful of my words. I will count to ten and not declare my war. I will count to ten and I will return to my father's house. I count to ten, sleep in, take a nap: these are tiny gifts of grace, O God, and there are many more.

Make well

I am cat. I make well. I am no doctor but I can heal. Let me sleep at your feet and you will know the difference. I can slow a racing heart. I can quiet a heavy spirit. I can even rhythms of the heart that waken you. I am cat and I heal. I have no medical credentials but doctors will mention me to you. Ask them about cat. I notice when you hurt and move slow. I know the sound of a sickroom and will come to you on tiptoe. On the bed I will make sure I should be there also. You lie still, I lie still. You stretch, I stretch. You open your eyes, I open my eyes. We stay, close, careful, still. It is bright daylight, you sleep, and then I will sleep more. I hear your breath. You die; I mourn. I will hunt your spirit in every room. I will not let you leave me. Grace keeps me at your side.

God, *how easy it is for me to show compassion. How quickly I will walk on tiptoe, keep a room quiet and make a spirit calm. How fast I serve someone who needs healing. God, you give me words to heal and to make well; you tell me when not to speak, how to whisper and how to touch. You have made me a caring person to do what I have been taught to do. A cat has taught me, as have my father and aunt and grandmother and mother and nurse. I feel the healing hands and gentle paws of all who would make me well. How soon they come running with medicines and balloons, comforters and roses and cool water and hot tea to a bedside. Grace is your credential of a healing spirit moving in and through us. A touch, a little oil, the laying on of hands, silence, a blessing, a massage, a hug, a right word—these make well. Grace is forever and ever.*

Tease

I am cat. I have a sense of humor; I surprise, I

tease. I have my way of making
a joke. I smile and I laugh as cat. I
jump from my hiding place and attack
your shoes; you jump. I did not hurt
you; sometimes we laugh at the same time. I hear
you. You bend down to pick me up, I dash away and
escape. I look back and laugh. We laugh together.
You dangle a toy above me and I keep my eyes shut.
I am peeking and waiting; preparing to tease. You think
I am too tired, then I leap into the air and catch the toy
and you scream. I surprised you. This is my joke, my sense
of humor. You say words like "cute" and "sweetheart" and I feel your tone
of voice; I know you like being teased. It is not the first time we have done
this together. I tease you because we like the surprise and the laughter.
If I hurt you I did not mean to. Grace is sometimes a very good joke, a
surprise, and a toy just out reach.

God, *how did you make us to tease one another? We surprise each other with a turn of the eye, turn of* a meaning, a gesture, and a laugh. How quickly we can be surprised. A bud on a tree makes us smile, if the limb is covered with snow. You tease us with early sprigs of grass, a sudden flock of birds honking overhead and a lawn of yellow chickadees rising in sudden flight. We smile and we laugh when a double rainbow arcs our house. We tease and surprise children so they tumble and hide and peek and do tricks while we run for cameras to capture moments of surprise. How playful is your grace; we stay your children all our years. We walk an old path and it is like new. We bend to touch what we did not see before. Wind dances a leaf mid air and we stop to stare. God, we find your grace in toys and jokes and somersaults and surprise. God, you tease. There are tiny times when I feel you are putting me on. Grace is fun, some- times just out of reach, sometimes like a riddle or a profound joke.

Look at me

I am cat. Look at me when you talk. See me

stare when I want you to help, to let me out, to give me dinner. I keep my
eyes on you because I am cat and cats must see your face. I notice your
eyes, your smile, your look, the sound of your words. I can see from below
if you are looking back or acting as if I am not there. You cannot hide your
face from a cat. I will come close and tell you what I feel when you are not

hearing, not feeling, not doing. I am cat and
I know your face, your hands and feet,
your heart. Look at me so you know I
am here. Grace will find the face.

God, *you do not hide your face from me for I am yours. You see me from afar and from within. You see*

where I was and where I will be. Help me to see you seeing me so I feel how close we are in the dark, in a storm, in fear or grief, and when there is nothing I hear but silence. You see me with a soft wind, bowing willows, people in prayer and angels who guard. Help me see your grace in the face and hands and faces lifted up in thanks and intercession. O God, open my eyes to see your eyes and to see the endless ways you look at me. Your grace means we see each other.

Satisfied

I am cat. I am easy to please. Sometimes I want just a crumb of a cookie, or I need one pat, one look, one word, one catnip toy. When I am satisfied then I am best at being cat. I purr, snuggle, stay at your feet, stretch out on the rug. I will do as I please. I do not need

expensive toys to make me glad. A string, a walnut, paper bag, marble, twig, tree, treat. A spoonful, a few drops, a morsel will be enough. I need to feel you are there, that you know I am here. Being present is my greatest pleasure. I learn to know the sound of your voice to know my own name. I am not jealous. I am cat. I have enough; we all have enough together. Grace is plentiful; I am satisfied.

God, *I am satisfied. You need not give me more to please me. My world is full. I need time to open your gifts and share them. My wants are few. Sometimes my wants are meager and basic: a good chair, a loaf of bread, a bowl of soup, a drink, a candle, and a friend. There are times when I am easily pleased: a kind word, a touch, work, a wave, a walk, a robin, a train whistle, an apple. Each of these is a feast. I am satisfied. Life is full. Like the cat one catnip toy is enough. One good word and I purr. A morsel, one smell of a bakery, one cluster of lilacs, one spring violet, a warbler, a bell, two children running, a family coming early to church and I am fulfilled. God, I am easy to please. I read one line in a song, I feel satisfied.*

"It is a gift to be simple." Grace is simple and grace makes free.

Care

I am cat. I know when I am sick. I will not eat,
I will not indulge. I hide and rest to save my strength. While I sleep and
doze I listen to my body; from my birth I have nurtured my health. There is
a lot a cat can do before calling 911. You are my 911 and my ambulance.
You help when there is nothing more I can do. I am cat and know how to
be well. I do not read health magazines or phone in sick. I was taught from
the beginning to know myself. From birth my mother said to me "Know
Thyself." It is an old saying among cats. When I am sick you offer me care.
I do the same to you for caring is an old rule of grace.

God, *I know my body. There is a lot I can do before calling 911. Growing well is also my work. Stretching, upper body, lower body, bending, reaching, touching toes: I know these; I have heard and done them. It is up to me to care for myself and for others. God, you have filled me with medicines of wellness. In my mind I see images of healing. In the Psalms you show me sickness and health and I am comforted. You help me picture the look of growing well. I can see light at the end of a tunnel, a candle in the dark, a song in very still night. I know and I obey. All nature declares your light and glory. Your mountains make me well. The cat gives me lessons in caring for each other and myself. I will learn from your whole creation.*

God, you give creation the power to care. This is your grace.

Washing

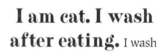

I am cat. I wash after eating. I wash when I have been in the rain. I wash when seeds and burrs cling to my fur. I am made to be clean. It is how I was taught when a kitten. My mother washed my face, behind my ears, myself. She cleaned me with strength when I was barely born and her tongue was her strong washcloth. I did not hear the words "Cleanliness is next to Godliness" but they are written in my genes. When my paws have walked through mud I will leave my prints on the floor and on a rug, wipe my feet clean with my tongue. It is the best I can do and I will do so without a command. I am cat; I like clean feet. You like a clean floor. You wash me in scented soap and dry me with a clean towel. You are proud of me. You are gracious to me; I am clean. My mother is right: "Cleanliness is next to Godliness."

God, *when I am unclean you wash me and I am whiter than snow. I pray to be clean, you show me how;* this is your promise to me. In the beginning I was washed, clean. With care I was bathed. Again I was washed in a font. Every bath is a reminder of the font. How often I too have said: Do not wash me. Then you washed me from head to foot; you washed me clean. I walked in the rain, and stayed. I am washed. I washed in a river. It is my turn to be in the Jordan. I am washed. I bowed, I knelt. I was buried in sorrow; you lifted me up. I am washed. I read Psalms, sang old hymns, confessed; I am washed. I ask that you create in me a clean heart; you renew a right spirit within me. Wash me with hyssop and I will be whiter than snow. God, old grace makes me clean.

A higher being

I am cat. I follow you, sit by you, purr when you look at me; I look up to you. You keep me fed, make me safe, call me by my name, open the door and let me in. You do what I cannot do. You are greater than I and I do not clearly comprehend magnificence. You have earned my trust and loyalty. You give me what I cannot reach or do on my own. You open cans, pour milk, give me

a blanket, open and close doors and give me a name. Did you create the trees I climb, the rain I watch from the porch, the sun that warms me and the snowflakes I chase? I did not make these so surely you did. How did you create the squirrels I chase and the dog next door and a mouse? Who helped you make the hill I run and the warm rock I stretch out on in summer? How did you make the butterfly I can never catch and the bird taunting me from the high branch? You are taller than I, greater and higher. I need you to look up to.

God, *I am not the highest. You are and I need a higher being. So I look up and see beyond myself. I give glory and feel myself lifted up, exalted. I need someone outside myself and family to give thanks. Someone to esteem. I will stay in wonder and awe; I will marvel and bow and see beyond the end. I will trust and not comprehend; believe and commit myself. May I stay in the miracle of mystery and see every blade of grass, each bud, hear each song of bird, know each aroma of bread and savor all raindrops as signs of your holiness. So may I obey you with speech and eyes and walk and will. Draw me to yourself through hope and dreams and faith. I will find you in my neighbor where you show me your grace.*

I know my place

I am cat. I know my place.

I only do what I am able to do. I will do what
you do if you teach me. I know many things to
do by heart. I know I may not sit in any place I
choose; there are places forbidden and I will need
to be reminded. Not every bed is mine and there
are rooms I will never see. I am curious as I see you
go in and shut the door and leave me standing.
If you shut the door hard I learn it is not my
place. Being cat makes me even more curious. I
try to honor your rules. Sometimes I feel it is our house, but it is clear I am
a boarder or perhaps a visitor. No, really, I am a member of your family. I
am cat and know where I belong and to whom.

God, *I belong. I am a member of a great people. I am not your whole body but I am a member, a child, a citizen of your kingdom, your family. I cannot be all things and not all gifts are mine. The days of life may not seem finished and a lifetime may seem too brief. You give me my time and my place. There were others before me and there are many yet to come. We all have our own time in your vineyard and our place at your one table. We pluck the harvest side by side; we pass the food to one another. I am one; this is enough for me to do. Show me the towel of Jesus and I will show others your good grace.*

I tread lightly

I am cat. Sometimes I go on tiptoe; I tread lightly. I can walk on thin ice and not break through. I can walk like the sound of mist, thick fog, a cloud in slow motion. My feet barely touch the earth when I walk in silence. Not a leaf stirs; I do not feel the stones beneath my paws. I walk as on cotton if I want and my feet float. It is a habit I have from the beginning: to tread lightly, to be sure and not walk into a trap for I too have predators. I know there are snares to catch me that I cannot untangle. I am cat, I tread lightly. Often I cannot hear myself, not even breathe, while I see and feel all around me, sensing. There is nothing I will not hear, but I do not hear my own heart beat. This was

taught me long ago and has saved me; stay calm. To tread lightly has given me extra lives. By treading lightly I may have not nine lives but twelve, for I am cat.

God, *you made life tender. Some days we walk as on thin ice, whisper, breathe lightly and listen. The days are not alike; some times are tender. Your word is old and change- less and yet you are new. Some words march, some tread lightly, some are as silent as an evening breeze; some of your words unfold slowly like an early blossom. Grace senses. There are snares that we avoid, mines we walk around, and emergency rooms in which we are qui- et and there are the wounded with whom we are patient. There are feuds to which we only listen and do not speak. We too can be drawn into a trap, or not. Grace sometimes treads firmly, sometimes like on soft paws, barefoot. Grace knows the textures, the feelings of hearts; grace wants not to bring harm or to be harmed. Grace is gracious.*

Talk to me

I am cat. Talk to me.

You do not need to meow or change your voice. Talk to me as though I am here with you, present with you, beside you. Do not be silent as though I do not need your words. Sometimes it is your turn to speak first, and then I will be sure to answer. Your silence makes me think you are busy, too busy. Silence can make me wonder if it was something I took that was not mine. I am cat, talk to me. I know what you mean. I understand by how fast you speak, if you look my way; touch me, how loud you talk, why you ask a question. These are clear to me. A long silence is hard to hear. Then I think thoughts that are not true and I feel feelings you do not have. I too like facts, the truth. If you want to be alone, tell me; tell me twice; then I will join your silence. If you want quiet show me. You know how much of my life is silence, resting, curling quiet on a pillow. I am cat, every day talk to me, just you and me.

God, *you are a conversing God. You talk and listen, you watch and sing; we sing and watch, we listen and talk. You have said your words as music and prayer and prophecies and blessing. Your voice has been heard on mountains, in caves, on deserts, in sleep, in temples, in battle, in gardens. For long you have spoken with us your children. We have debated, obeyed, asked, agreed, bargained and memorized your commands. Your voice is loud and very clear. Then you are so still; time passes; there is no voice of the Lord. You give me time; I ponder what you have already said. I remember what I have read and heard. Speak to me in person; speak through others in scripture, in my family, in this world now.*

You are not a silent God. Grace is a conversation.

Good morning

I am cat. I think it is time for us to get up. You do not need an alarm clock; you have me. I can wake you in person, however you want: with a purr, a lick, a nuzzle, walking on your body, breathing in your face. There are many ways to wake you. I have wakened and stretched, said my thanks, tiptoed, sat blinking; now it is time for all to waken for I am wide awake and there is a good day ahead. Birds are singing, the sun is high, I see a squirrel; the house is too quiet. Good morning. You need to eat; I cannot make you breakfast but I can wake you, so I have. I would never wake you with the loud ring of the alarm. I wake you with my soft fur, purring, a joyful meow and massaging your body with my paws. I am cat; good morning. O day full of grace.

God, *I wake in morning again and again in so many good ways: rain against the window, sunshine in the face, still dark, thick fog all around, snow blowing, a waft of spring aroma through the open window. This is how I wake. Thank you. Come, O day full of grace. Sometimes I am waked by a cat jumping on the bed, purring and pawing; sometimes the smell of coffee brewing, a door slam, the alarm, a child's voice, or just waking again on time. Thank you. Come, O day full of grace. How often I wake to a new day, a long journey, work, a holiday, a friend at the door, birds in a tree outside the window. Thank you. Come, O day full of grace. Awake, eyes wide open; time to dream, a heart full of hope, and a mind full of imagination, ready. Thank you. Come, O day full of grace. A thump on the bed, purring, pawing, breathing, a sure sign of life; breath, breath of God calling me through a cat. Get up; this is the day the Lord has made. Be glad in it. I am. I am awake.*

Grace means good morning.

I believe

I am cat. I believe. I do
not need printed creeds; I do not
recite presidential addresses or sing
national anthems. I only believe. I
believe in staring at a sunset, noticing
the wind blowing and focus my sight on
weeping willows dancing an evening
breeze. My eyes will take a thousand
photos of a sparrow on a high wire.

I believe in the magnificence of walking alone under a full
moon and seeing clouds make shadows on a midnight ground. I believe in
chasing a leaf dancing in autumn believing there is life in that red maple
being. The toys I like best are around me. I wonder at the feel of sand, the
slow motion of a snail, the speed of a hare and the comfort of a familiar
voice, the aroma of the same pillow. Some believe with all their heart. I am
cat; I believe with all my senses. Grace believes.

God, *your grace makes me a believer. Stars and sun and seasons and winter snow are gifts. When I believe*

I am sure; trust and faith are your gifts to me. When I believe I see and hear. When I believe I will stare at sunsets, recite psalms, sing hymns, and stay to watch a weeping willow bud, bloom and green and bow in a believer's dance. God, when I am bored with unbelief send clouds and sparrow songs to help my believing. When I am tired of family, afraid of death and lost in pity help my unbelief. When I miss the budding of red maples and do not find time to hear a child singing help my unbelief. I too watch the sparrow on a high wire and feel my credo; I feel salvation when singing "nestling bird nor star in heaven / such a refuge e'er was given." I believe when I eat oatmeal, pack my children's lunch, smell a casserole, pour wine, light candles, pass the peace, rise to sing, study a stained glass window. Your universe is filled with one grace. Any sign of grace will help my unbelief.

God, you made me to believe so I believe.

Routine

I am cat. Am I consistent? I like repetition, a routine. There are paths I follow by heart. My paths are marked like a map; my routines are predictable. You see me do them day after day and you smile, as though I do not know. You follow me in the night and know my ways. There is a way I am used to. I do not like changing a habit I have begun. I have ways that work and I know them. Routines fit me and all that is around me. I am cat and I know my place. I do not like a door suddenly closed so I will lose my path. I know the schedule you keep; I know the bedroom, bathroom, kitchen, stove, refrigerator, table, sink. Each day

we walk through our routines together in these places. I am cat; you know me by my habits. Depend on me. I do not live in a rut. I live on a way. I am cat; I have a way; you have a way. It is our way together.

God, *there is a way, a path I follow by heart. It is like a chart, a map in me. It is a guide by day and in the* dark. The path is more than routine, more than a habit; I am a pilgrim and I walk a traveled route. There are signs of ancestors and saints before me; I see the marks and chapels and cathedrals and crosses of martyrs. The names of apostles and holy sites are near and far. The road is old and sometimes new. I follow this way with my heart and mind and it fits my feet, my family and my friends. I am on a faith walk, sometimes alone, often with many. We stop to talk and read and rest along the way. When I am tired, there is a bed; if sick there is help. When sad, there is a singer. Some of the paths are too steep. God, you know the side roads marked closed. I try them. I am learning to know the way. I am glad to see the pilgrims. None are missing. Some are running; some are very slow, singing, dancing, praising.

This is your way of grace.